Unit

Long Vowel Express

MW00571783

Mc Graw Hill Education

Contents

Nate and Pam

Nate and Mom can name it.

Pam and Dad came to it.

Nate and Pam can tame it.

Pam can pat the mane.

Nate and Pam can tape it.

The Ape Ate It

leonp69/iStock/Getty Images

See a tame ape.

An ape came to a mate.

Can I see the same ape?

A man in tan came in.

The ape ate on top.

A Ripe Lime

The lime is ripe.
You can pick it.

Pick a fat ripe lime.
You can tap a fat lime.

Pick a fine pile.
Set ten in a line.

Sam can bite on a lime.
Rob can sip it.

I like a ripe lime.

Ride, Hike, Hide

Photo by Jason Weddington/
Moment Open/Getty Images

I can ride a red bike.
I can sit on it!

I can hop in.
I can not ride in it!

I can hike a mile.
I can hide.

I can not hit a big hive.
I can not hide in time!

I can kick it a lot.
I can hit it fine!

Jack Rode Up

Rex rode in a big jet.
It rose up.
Rex got home.

Jo did the job.

Jo got the rope up.

See the big dome, Jo?

27

Thomas Northcut/Photodisc/Getty Images

Jan rose up to the top.
Jan did not doze.
Jan did like it!

Jack got in and hit ten.
So, Jack rode up.
Jack rode to the top.

Gus got in line.
He rode up.
Gus can go back!

Hope Rode Home

The sun rose.

Hope can go see Kim Mole.

"Home at sunset!" said Mom.

Hope rode to Kim.
Hope was hot.
Hope and Kim ate a cone.

33

Kim Mole had a rope.
"Let us hop," said Hope.
Hope and Kim had fun!

Kim had a red hose.
A hose can wet a rose.
Kim did not get Hope wet!

Hope had to go home.
So, Hope rode up the lane.
Hope got home at sunset!

Nate and Pam   WORD COUNT: 32

DECODABLE WORDS   HIGH-FREQUENCY WORDS
Target Phonics Elements   **Review:** and, the, to
Long *a, a_e:* came, mane, name,
Nate, tame, tape

The Ape Ate It   WORD COUNT: 31

DECODABLE WORDS   HIGH-FREQUENCY WORDS
Target Phonics Elements   **Review:** a, I, see, the, to
Long *a, a_e:* ape, ate, came, mate,
same

A Ripe Lime   WORD COUNT: 46

DECODABLE WORDS   HIGH-FREQUENCY WORDS
Target Phonics Elements   **Review:** a, is, you
Long *i, i_e:* bite, fine, like, lime, line,
pile, ripe

Ride, Hike, Hide   WORD COUNT: 56

DECODABLE WORDS   HIGH-FREQUENCY WORDS
Target Phonics Elements   **Review:** a, I
Long *i, i_e:* bike, fine, hide, hike,
hive, mile, ride, time

Jack Rode Up   WORD COUNT: 69

DECODABLE WORDS   HIGH-FREQUENCY WORDS
Target Phonics Elements   **Review:** a, and, he, see, the, to
Long *o,* Spelled *o_e, o:* dome, doze,
home, rode, rope, rose, go, Jo, so

Hope Rode Home   WORD COUNT: 78

DECODABLE WORDS   HIGH-FREQUENCY WORDS
Target Phonics Elements   **Review:** a, and, said, see, the,
Long *o,* Spelled *o_e, o:* cone, home,   to, was
Hope, hose, Mole, rode, rope, rose,
go, so

37

HIGH-FREQUENCY WORDS TAUGHT TO DATE

Grade K	Unit 8
	a
Unit 4	and
a	are
and	can
can	do
do	for
go	go
I	have
like	he
see	here
the	I
to	is
we	like
you	little
	me
Unit 6	my
a	of
and	said
are	see
can	she
do	the
go	they
he	this
I	to
is	want
like	was
little	we
my	what
see	with
she	you
the	
to	
was	
we	
with	
you	

DECODING SKILLS TAUGHT TO DATE

UNIT 4
Initial and final consonant *m*; short *a*; initial *s*; initial and final consonant *p*; initial and final consonant *t*; initial and medial vowel *i*; initial and final consonant *n*; initial *c*; initial and medial vowel *o*; initial and final *d*

UNIT 6
Initial and final consonant *m*; short *a*; initial *s*; initial and final consonant *p*; initial and final consonant *t*; initial and medial vowel *i*; initial and final consonant *n*; initial *c*; initial and medial vowel *o*; initial and final *d*; initial consonant *h*; initial and medial vowel *e*; initial consonants *f* and *r*; initial and final consonant *b*; initial consonant *l*; initial consonant *k*; final digraph *ck*

UNIT 8
Initial and final consonant *m*; short *a*; initial *s*; initial and final consonant *p*; initial and final consonant *t*; initial and medial vowel *i*; initial and final consonant *n*; initial *c*; initial and medial vowel *o*; initial and final *d*; initial consonant *h*; initial and medial vowel *e*; initial consonants *f* and *r*; initial and final consonant *b*; initial consonant *l*; initial consonant *k*; final digraph *ck*; initial and medial vowel *u*; initial and final *g*; initial *w*; final consonant *x*; initial consonant *v*; initial consonant *j*; initial consonant *qu*; initial consonant *z*; initial consonant *y*